Don't Dis Miss!

Soem pomes

By
Ian Billings

Illustrated by Debbie Slater

contains daft language throughout

Starring
(in alphabetical order)

A,B,C,D,E,F,G,H,I,J,K,L,
M,N,O,P,Q,R,S,T,U,V,W,X,Y,Z

D1321881

For Izzy, Billy, Meg and Fi

Written by
IAN BILLINGS

First Published
January 07. in Great Britain by

PUBLISHING

© **Ian Billings 2007**

The moral right of the author has been asserted in accordance with the
Copyright, Designs and Patents Act 1988

A CIP record for this work is available from the British Library

ISBN-10: 1-905637-11-X
ISBN-13: 978-1-905637-11-9

Typeset by Educational Printing Services Limited

Educational Printing Services Limited
Unit 6, Glenfield Park 2, Northrop Avenue, Blackburn BB1 5QH
Telephone: (01254) 686500   Fax: (01254) 686501
E-mail: enquiries@eprint.co.uk   Website: www.eprint.co.uk

Contents

© IAN BILLINGS

Subject to condition

This book is sold subject to the condition,
It will not be copied without permission,
Or sat on or stolen or worn as a hat,
Or pages torn out and fed to the cat.

Without the publishers prior consent,
It cannot be spat on or dropped in cement.
And don't go shoving it down the loo,
'cos the publisher'll do the same to you.

BEE

Look what's happened to me
I've just been stung by a bee
It seems an awful lot of money
£20 for a jar of honey.

The Seal

Chocolate animal biscuits.
I adore them – there's
Giraffes, lions, tigers,
Penguins and there's bears.

The supermarket was beckoning me,
So I bought a pack today.
But suddenly I stopped and stared
Whilst on my way to pay

I read the packet carefully,
I'm always quiet precise.
It was then I saw a notice
That really caught my eyes.

I hurried down the shopping aisle.
Packet clutched in hand.
I couldn't stop or wait a while
To enjoy my favourite brand.

But the notice had upset me,
I had to know the truth.
I waited for the manager
to come out of his booth.

I shouted at the manager
(Now I wish I hadn't spoken)
"Is it true I can't eat this food -
if the seal is broken?"

The Monster in the Hallway

Here it bursts right through the door,
Hear it snarling, hear it roar.
Scowling, frowning, yelling, yawning.
A scary sight on Monday morning.

It sniffs the air, it's teeth go crunch
It knows there's ravioli for lunch.
It walks the hall stalking prey
wishing for an indoor play.

"The Monsters loose inside the school!",
Watch them scatter through the drool.
Trying to avoid detection,
They hide themselves inside reception.

It licks the ground where a child fell
Then hisses at the morning bell.
It knows the children are all trembling
As in the hall they start assembling.

It follows them in, running wild,
Clawing at each frightened child
Chasing children, gnawing bones -
we simply call her Mrs. Jones.

Scented

My little brother, on Valentine's day
Came rushing down the hall.
Then I heard him, panting, say,
"For you a card, pink, quite small."

"Everywhere I wented
I ranned as fast as I canned!"
I said, "A Valentine's Card? Was it scented?"
He said, "No, delivered by hand!"

PROFESSIONAL WRITER

I'm a professional writer
Today I wrote the word "Mother"
I've refilled my pencil
And sharpened my pen –
So tomorrow I may write another.

PIE RECIPE

Take some pastry, three months old,
Check it's rotten and covered with mold.
Cover the base of a baking tin
And then put the following ingredients in –
Some sweepings from a barbers shop,
anything you might find in a mop.
Some cold custard, a used tissue,
Yellow snow and some rabbit poo.
A large portion of old dandruff,

Ingredients

3 month old mouldy pastry

baking tin

barber's shop sweepings

mop bits

cold custard

used tissue

yellow snow

rabbit poo

old dandruff

ear wax

belly button fluff

old cotton buds

used toothpaste

half a teaspoon of light grey dust

cardboard crust

handful of snot

long dead worm

A pinch of ear wax and belly button fluff.
Stir in a teaspoon of bathroom waste –
Old cottonbuds and used toothpaste,
Half a teaspoon of light grey dust
And then add on top the cardboard crust.
Garnish with a handful of snot
And bake for three days 'til it's nice and hot.
Top it off with a long dead worm
And serve to your teacher
on the last day of term.

Punk-tuation

Why can't we hear all the commas?
Why is a full-stop quite mute?
What noise does a ! make?
This really doesn't compute.

When you read a good piece of writing,
You listen for every word –
But I have a proclamation -
It's time punctuation was heard!

Let's give voice to a colon
Let's make a noise for a stop.
An apostrophe yearns for a yelling.
Let's make literacy hop!

Dashes, hashes, forward-slashes,
Hyphens could go twang,
Apostrophes could yodel
And asterisks go clang!

Ber-doing go a couple of brackets,
Kerrang go quotation marks,
@ signs probably tinkle
Sound bites as bad as their barks.

History will show we're not stupid
We've invented a brand new art
Ellipsis could sound like sneezes
And a full-stop could sound like a –

Part of the new generation
Of people speaking this way.
Make punctuation noisy.
Run out and try it today!

On telly later tonight

On telly later tonight,
There's plenty of stuff to delight.
Two dogs in pyjamas,
Whilst eating bananas
And a bishop flying a kite.

There's a partly political broadcast,
And a cat with the weather forecast,
A ship wrapped in foil,
The queen eating soil.
And a musical Elastoplast.

At ten a programme on warts.
Then a rabbit shares his thoughts,
On the state of the world,
Why his lettuce has curled,
And how good he looks in pink shorts.

We've a programme on jumping in puddles,
And some aardvarks sitting in huddles
Cookery, too.
A man eats his shoe.
And the Prime Minister appeals for more cuddles.

There's dribbling for the beginner,
A postman sits in his dinner,
Two chat show hosts,
Climb up some posts
And a ferret says both are the winner.

But it's all a lie you see
None of it's on TV.
It's just been invented
By an announcer, demented.
You really must excuse,
I did it to amuse.
I'm easily bored
I should be ignored
Sorry about that – here's the news.

Beware! Take Care!

Our school care-taker, Mr. Mole
Didn't take care - so he fell in a hole.

When your job's about taking care,
If there's a hole in the ground you should beware.

(PS – Don't worry about the hole in the ground – the police
are looking into it.)

Mrs. Malcolm

Mrs. Malcolm had a theory
On how to keep her pupils cheery.
She gave them custard, jam and honey
And bribed each one with eggs (quite runny.)
To keep them happy she gave them sweets,
"There's a prize for everyone who cheats!
For copying there's a giant cake –
And a carrot for every rule you break!
For missing school I'll give a toffee
- and for a mummy a jar of coffee."

Mrs. Malcolm had a letter
Telling her to do much better.
Then she had to see the Head –
Whom most approached with fear and dread.
But Mrs. Malcolm knocked the door
And gaily skipped across the floor.
He told her, as his face turned green
"You're the worst teacher I've ever seen.
The way you teach makes me wail –
Each and every child will fail!"
A look of joy then crossed her eyes
And she simply said, "So where's my prize?"

It really was an awful to do -
But don't you wish Mrs. Malcolm taught you?

Limerick

There was a young girl from Kilcady,
Who had a delightful young body
But after ten years
Of peanuts and beers
She now looks a lot like Bill Oddie.

LIMERICK

(instrumental version)

Da-diddley-diddley-diddle.
Da-diddley-diddley-diddle.
Da-diddley-dah,
Da-diddley-dah,
Da-diddley-diddley-diddle.

(Put in your own words – I've had a hard day)

Keep Your Distance

"Keep your Distance"
says the sign
on the motorway.

But I do keep my distance.
I keep it in a box.
It's a very long box.

It...

Hide it in your rough book,
Don't let teacher see it.
Put it in your pencil case,
Don't let teacher see it.

Slip it in your lunch box,
Don't let teacher see it.
Put it in your pocket,
But don't let teacher see it.

Lose it in your PE kit,
Hide it be a mate,
Don't let teacher see it.
Oh, oh! Oh, no! Too late!

I'm a Poet

Gurgle, furgle, wurgle, flob,
Urgle, turgle, murgle, zob.
Flishy, flushy, mushy, tob.
I'm a poet – it's a funny sort of job.

Holiday

I'm going away for a holiday.
I'm not sailing or going by rail.
I've found a far more cheaper way
I'm travelling by Royal Mail.

I wrote the address on my hairy chest
And stuck a big stamp on my nose.
I've tied my bags to my nice string vest
Will I get there do you suppose?

Hobbies

I've come to a final conclusion
Hobbies are a waste of time
They only cause confusion
And mess up your leisure time.

The horse club I joined dismounted
The running club just didn't start.
The maths society was discounted
And the human pyramid fell apart.

I was dropped by the parachuting club
They asked me back but I refused
So I joined a bomb making club
But that was soon diffused

I was in a hairdressing club for a bit,
It was my favourite, it mattered,
But they parted and finally split.
The chicken feeding club simply scattered.

The wood cutting club was whittled away
The sailing club went adrift
The Tuesday Club changed its day
I was becoming really miffed.

But the most depressing thing
That I was ever told
my favourite origami club
was going to have to fold.

SPROUT

"What's it all about?"
thought the lonely little sprout,
sitting on the canteen tray.

"I wonder what the use is
sitting in my juices,
hoping to be whisked away."

"I wish I were a chip,
covered all in dip
not just cold and old debris."

But all that grease
Makes kids obsese
I'm glad I'm just little old me.

THE GREAT EXPLORER

"I am the finest specimen of human exploration,
I'll announce my next achievement with this jolly declaration
Throughout the world they all declare there's simply no one greater –
And so I announce my thrilling quest - I plan to climb the equator!

Once I've conquered that small task, I'll try something more romantic
I'll take a herd of a hundred goats and walk across the Atlantic.
I'll ski across the Sahara Desert then the mighty Red Sea I'll hike,
Followed by my greatest feat to traverse the Med on a bike.

I'm planning to cross the Congo, underwater by balloon.
After that I'm going to be the first submariner on the moon
Then I'll jump off Everest with a parachute made from a map."
Then a nurse touched his shoulder and said "I think its time
for your nap."

DOOR

Dad took our front door
back to the DIY store.
He was angry, in a fit.
"Why bring back your door
back to our DIY store?
It's odd I have to admit."

"I brought back this door
to your DIY store,
I'm so angry I could spit,
I brought back this door
to your DIY store,
'cos someone's already opened it!"

1,2,3

1,2,3 were very scared
when they sat down to dine.
4,5,6 were frightened too,
because 7 ate 9.

Bouncy castle

In the bouncy castle
Lived the bouncy king and queen
And their bouncy little daughter
Princess Maureen.

They bounced all day
And most of the night
Bounced through the weekend
It was quite a sight.

But Princess Maureen
Soon got bored.
And hatched a plan
While her parents snored.

She rummaged around
And found a pin
Went to their bedroom
And bounced quietly in.

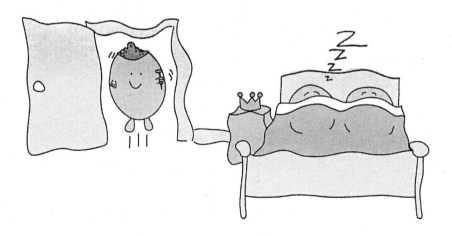

Over to the bed
With a bo-ing and hop
She pricked papa
And pop went pop

Mama woke and spoke
With a frown
"I think you've let
your father down."

"It won't happen again,
I do declare!"
Declared the princess
But that was all hot-air.

Between you and me
Her chances are blown
of ever inheriting
the bouncy throne.

WORDS

After the nativity parents gather in herds
And the head teacher stands "to say a few words."

All went quiet through respect for the head
But on this occasion this is what she said,

"Oyster, jam jar, pokemon, cheese,
flotsam, jetsam, wobbling, knees,
Pog, pencils, a dollop of jam,
Dimple, wimple, call me Pam.

Bedlam, French fries, top trumps, gunge,
Hocus pocus, trembling, plunge,
Flabby, dodgy, a giant brolly,
Pimple, crimple, call me Molly!"

A feeling a doom
Ran around the room
The parents had expected
All the words to be connected.

"I'm all of a tizzy. I'm a head in a spin,
I'll explain it all, but where to begin?
Oh, deary me, I should be beheaded –
I'm all of a dither 'cos we're being ofstedded!"

THE TEACHER™

OPERATING INSTRUCTIONS

Thank you for purchasing **THE TEACHER**™· Please follow the following fully.

KEY FEATURES

1 Sees things in your pocket like gum or elastic
2 Beware of this part may be loud or sarcastic
3 Can hear things up to ten metres away.
4 May need wiping on a very cold day.
5 Can be greasy, oily or dry
6 Can't play football but will often try
7 Skin comes smooth or smothered with zits.
8 Beware of these fast moving bits.

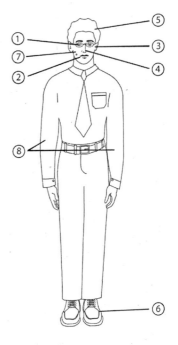

DANGER

DO NOT ATTEMPT TO REMOVE THE COVER OR LOOK AT THE WORKINGS.

INSTALLING YOUR TEACHER™

Unpack, very carefully then place on a chair,
(Make sure no one's left a drawing pin there) –
Remove the coat, the scarf and the hat,
Then wind-up your **TEACHER**™ and hear it chat.

 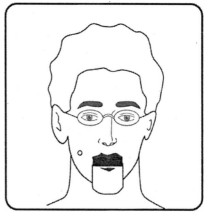

NEVER WIND-UP YOUR **TEACHER**™ TOO MUCH.
IT MAY CAUSE DAMAGE.

CARING FOR YOUR TEACHER™

Wipe only with a dampish rag
And if your **TEACHER**™ starts to sag
Pat its head and then insert
A spoonful of a nice dessert

 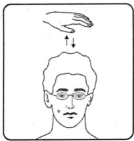 

CLOSING DOWN YOUR TEACHER™

To close down your **TEACHER**™ is very simple,
You have to locate its on/off dimple.
But wait until the end of the day,
Give it a prod – and then run away.

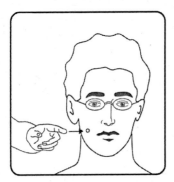

<u>MOST IMPORTANT</u> [WARNING]

KEEP YOUR TEACHER™ OUT OF THE REACH OF CHILDREN
FIRST THING IN THE MORNING.

Karaoke Poetry!

This book is now available as an audio CD for your very own ears.
You can read along with your favourite poems!
Featuring Ian Billings and his mouth!
If you don't like Ian Billings reading the poems, simply play the
CD, place your fingers in your ears and read them yourself!
Free hole in the middle with every purchase!

Order on-line **www.eprint.co.uk**